Busy, Busy Bees Clean Up!

By JONATHAN PEALE

Illustrated by TOM HEARD

Music Arranged and Produced by DREW TEMPERANTE

MATTESON AREA PUBLIC LIBRARY DISTRICT

CANTATA
LEARNING

WWW.CANTATALEARNING.COM

CANTATA
LEARNING

Published by Cantata Learning
1710 Roe Crest Drive
North Mankato, MN 56003
www.cantatalearning.com

A note to educators and librarians from the publisher: Cantata Learning has provided the following data to assist in book processing and suggested use of Cantata Learning product.

Publisher's Cataloging-in-Publication Data
Prepared by Librarian Consultant: Ann-Marie Begnaud
Library of Congress Control Number: 2015958181
    Busy, Busy Bees Clean Up!
    Series: School Time Songs
    Retold by Jonathan Peale
    Illustrated by Tom Heard
    Summary: A song that teaches students how to clean up their classroom.
    ISBN: 978-1-63290-613-7 (library binding/CD)
    ISBN: 978-1-63290-564-2 (paperback/CD)
Suggested Dewey and Subject Headings:
    Dewey: E 395.5
    LCSH Subject Headings: Courtesy – Juvenile literature. | Students – Juvenile literature. | Courtesy – Songs and music – Texts.
| Students – Songs and music – Texts. | Courtesy – Juvenile sound recordings. | Students – Juvenile sound recordings.
    Sears Subject Headings: Helping behavior. | Courtesy. | Students. | School songbooks. | Children's songs. | Popular music.
    BISAC Subject Headings: JUVENILE NONFICTION / School & Education. | JUVENILE NONFICTION / Music /
Songbooks. | JUVENILE NONFICTION / Social Topics / Values & Virtues.

Book design and art direction, Tim Palin Creative
Editorial direction, Flat Sole Studio
Music direction, Elizabeth Draper
Music arranged and produced by Drew Temperante

Printed in the United States of America in North Mankato, Minnesota.
072016   0335CGF16

ACCESS THE MUSIC!

SCAN CODE WITH MOBILE APP

CANTATALEARNING.COM

Busy bees work together to make honey. But "busy bee" can also mean someone who works hard. You and your classmates can work together like busy bees to keep your classroom clean and neat.

Now turn the page and sing along as you buzz around and clean up!

Oh, we're busy, busy bees,
and everyone agrees
Buzz, buzz!

that our room is nice and clean,
up and down and in between.
Buzz, buzz!

Oh, here's a messy mess,
messy mess.

Can we clean this mess?
Yes, yes, yes!

First we'll make some **plans**.
Then we'll use our busy hands!

Oh, we're busy, busy bees,
and everyone agrees
Buzz, buzz!

that our room is nice and clean,
up and down and in between.
Buzz, buzz!

Let's make things nice and neat,
nice and neat.

Cleaning is a treat,
is a treat!

We make things nice and neat,
just like bees make something sweet.

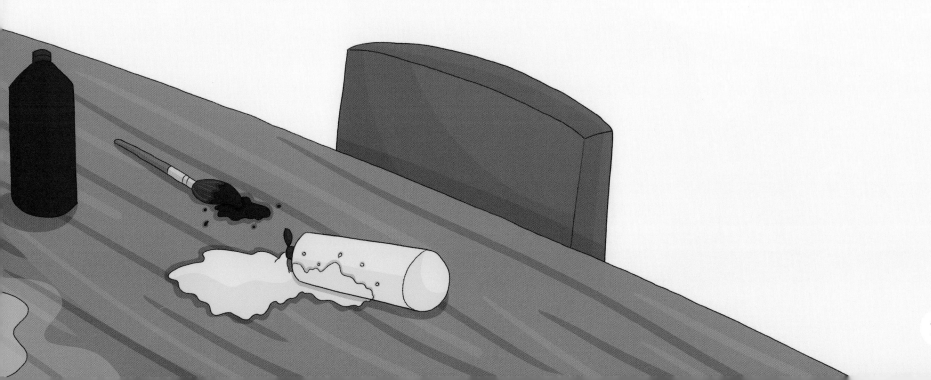

Oh, we're busy, busy bees,
and everyone agrees
    Buzz, buzz!

14

that our room is nice and clean,
up and down and in between.
Buzz, buzz!

Oh, we're busy, busy bees,
and everyone agrees
Buzz, buzz!

that our room is nice and clean,
up and down and in between.
Buzz, buzz!

Now everything is clean.

It's so clean,

perfect for a **queen**,

for a queen!

If there's a mess again,
we will clean it up, and then
it will be the cleanest room
you've ever seen!

Buzz, buzz!

21

SONG LYRICS
Busy, Busy Bees Clean Up!

Oh, we're busy, busy bees,
and everyone agrees
    Buzz, buzz!

that our room is nice and clean,
up and down and in between.
    Buzz, buzz!

Oh, here's a messy mess,
messy mess.
Can we clean this mess?
Yes, yes, yes!

First we'll make some plans.
Then we'll use our busy hands!

Oh, we're busy, busy bees,
and everyone agrees
    Buzz, buzz!

that our room is nice and clean,
up and down and in between.
    Buzz, buzz!

Let's make things nice and neat,
nice and neat.
Cleaning is a treat,
is a treat!

We make things nice and neat,
just like bees make something sweet.

Oh, we're busy, busy bees,
and everyone agrees
    Buzz, buzz!

that our room is nice and clean,
up and down and in between.
    Buzz, buzz!

Oh, we're busy, busy bees,
and everyone agrees
    Buzz, buzz!

that our room is nice and clean,
up and down and in between.
    Buzz, buzz!

Now everything is clean.
It's so clean,
perfect for a queen,
for a queen!

If there's a mess again,
we will clean it up, and then
it will be the cleanest room
you've ever seen!
    Buzz, buzz!

Busy, Busy Bees Clean Up!

Hip Hop (Americana)
Drew Temperante

Chorus

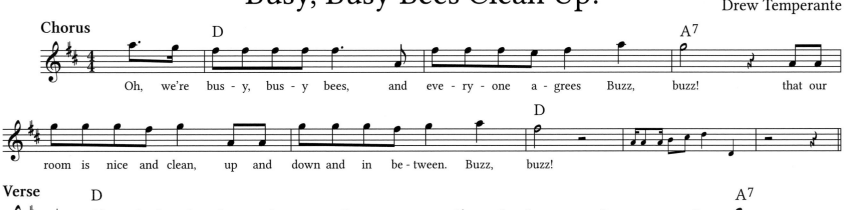

Oh, we're bus-y, bus-y bees, and eve-ry-one a-grees Buzz, buzz! that our

room is nice and clean, up and down and in be-tween. Buzz, buzz!

Verse

1. Oh, here's a mess-y mess, mess-y mess. Can we clean this mess? Yes, yes, yes!

First we'll make some plans. Then we'll use our bus-y hands!

Chorus

Verse 2
Let's make things nice and neat, nice and neat.
Cleaning is a treat, is a treat!
We make things nice and neat,
just like bees make something sweet.

Chorus

(Instrumental)

Chorus

Verse 3
Now everything is clean. It's so clean,
perfect for a queen, for a queen!
If there's a mess again,
we will clean it up, and then

Coda

it will be the clean-est room you've ev-er seen! Buzz, buzz!

GLOSSARY

plans—sets of actions to do something or make something happen

queen—a female ruler, also the member of a bee or ant colony that produces young

GUIDED READING ACTIVITIES

1. How do you help in your classroom? Do you help clean up, take care of a classroom pet, or help your teacher?

2. What would happen if things were always messy and dirty? How would that make you feel?

3. Chores are jobs you do almost every day, like keeping your room clean or helping set the table for dinner. What sorts of chores do you do at home?

TO LEARN MORE

Laffin, Jenna. *Let's Clean Up!* Mankato, MN: Cantata Learning, 2016.

Ponto, Joanna. *Being Respectful.* New York: Enslow, 2015.

Rissman, Rebecca. *Cleaning Up: Comparing Past and Present.* Mankato, MN: Heinemann-Raintree, 2014.

Smith, Sian. *Manners at School.* Mankato, MN: Heinemann-Raintree, 2013.